The Weed Garden

By Bill Early, Jr.

PublishAmerica
Baltimore

ISBN: 1-60672-201-8
PUBLISHED BY PUBLISHAMERICA, LLLP
www.publishamerica.com
Baltimore

Printed in the United States of America

To my wife Lois and all our family and friends who have encouraged us in our walk with God

Foreword

We reap what we sow.
Many of us unintentionally wind up with weeds instead of flowers
because we do not plant the right seed. We shy away from *"whatever is*
true, whatever is noble, whatever is right, whatever is pure,
whatever is lovely, whatever is admirable… excellent or
praiseworthy"—(Philippians 4:8)

Jesus told a parable in Matthew 13:

24 "The kingdom of heaven is like a man who sowed good seed in his field.
25 But while everyone was sleeping, his enemy came and sowed weeds
among the wheat, and went away. 26 When the wheat sprouted and formed
heads, then the weeds also appeared.
27 "The owner's servants came to him and said, 'Sir, didn't you sow good
seed in your field? Where then did the weeds come from?'
28 "'An enemy did this,' he replied.
"The servants asked him, 'Do you want us to go and pull them up?'
29 "'No,' he answered, 'because while you are pulling the weeds, you may
root up the wheat with them. 30 Let both grow together until the harvest. At
that time I will tell the harvesters: First collect the weeds and tie them in
bundles to be burned; then gather the wheat and bring it into my barn.'"

Good seed has been sown. But an enemy has sown tares among the wheat,
and now weeds abound! It is the will of God that both grow together until the
final harvest:

40 "As the weeds are pulled up and burned in the fire, so it will be at the end of the age. 41 The Son of Man will send out his angels, and they will weed out of his kingdom everything that causes sin and all who do evil. 42 They will throw them into the fiery furnace, where there will be weeping and gnashing of teeth. 43 Then the righteous will shine like the sun in the kingdom of their Father. He who has ears, let him hear."

The Weed Garden

I have a lovely garden 'round the edges of my yard;
But I don't plow the ground, or hoe, or bust up any clod.
And if, in Springtime, any pretty flowers start to show,
I pull them all up by the roots, so the weeds can grow!

No begonias, snapdragons, or tulips very nice,
No potatoes, lima beans, tomatoes, herbs or spice.
I'll settle for my tares and vetch, o'er there the poison ivy;
The crabgrass and the thistles are appearing very lively.

This always makes my neighbors chatter noisily, like birds:
"Don't you have it backwards, sir? Vice-versa, in other words?
Your garden is your future, to prepare for winter's dearth,
Should you not be planting corn and veggies in the earth?"

"It's very easy to explain," I tell them every season,
"What I want here is a crop of weeds, and here's the reason:
It takes far more effort raising all those useful plants,
And too much television time is wasted doing that.

"I'll be drinking sodas from my hammock in the shade;
Others will be toiling on, while I will have it made.

I will soon be snoozing while the diligent will sweat,
And they will one day wish they'd been as smart as me, I bet!

"What good are beans and melons when you have no time to play?
Why do the farmers bother? They just huff and puff all day.
Then they have to harvest all those food crops in the fall…
No, weeds are easier to raise; they take no work at all."

Each Autumn I get hungry from my head down to my feet,
And find to my dismay that there is not a crumb to eat.
So I go a-begging to my neighbors down the road,
Asking whether they have extra morsels they have growed.

Fast Food

I went to the fast-food plaza to dine
When business constraints cut into my time.
Seventeen people stood before me in line,
Each with nine kids with a penchant to whine.

They all wanted burgers and french fries and grease,
Things that cause zits and corrosive disease…
Some unholy teens were disturbing the peace…
One of them skateboarded into my knees.

Orders got bungled and needed redone;
A lady complained at the top of her lungs,
While her children, the brattiest under the sun,
Sniveled and yammered for a sesame bun.

Tho' sharp were the elbows, undaunted I stood,
Tapping my toes, all patient and good.
I glanced at my watch, in darkening mood…
And fought back the urge to grab somebody's food!

Before I could order, my lunch break had passed.
(The whole place was running on skeleton staff)…
Isn't it funny? Ya just have to laugh:
Eating "fast food" took an hour and a half.

The Pleasure Van

The Pleasure Van was filled with youths who took it for a weekend spin,
I would mention, their intention was to have a lick of sin.

The wind a-blowing through their hair made the young ones feel alive,
But come nightfall they would park it; that way, no one had to drive.

They parked it on a slight incline, overlooking Black Rock Cliff,
And quite unnnoticed by the rev'lers, Pleasure Van began to drift.

And while the partygoers drank and drugged their every care away,
The tires, ever slightly, turned as force of gravity held sway.

The spellbound youths could feel the bumping as the Pleasure Van did roll,
But they thought it was the drugs that made them bouncy, heart and soul.

Minutes passed, and Pleasure Van now moved much faster, gathering speed!
But those inside just strummed guitars, and sang that love is all we need.

Somebody should hit the brakes and stop that van before it plunged!
But nobody was interested; they all were having too much fun!

Soon the speeding Pleasure Van had passed the point of no returning.
Everything was over but the flailing, screaming, crashing, burning.

The Emperor and the Beggar

The beggar trod against the cold along the frozen road;
He forced his bare feet forward, as he clutched his tattered robe.
The hope that drove him onward, in spite of all his ills,
Was a warm and bright Inheritance across a hundred hills.

From the opposite direction came dragoons with sharpened lances,
And pushed the beggar man aside with sneering, haughty glances.
"Kneel before your betters, for the Emperor doth come!
Bow yer dirty face, ye cur, before his trav'ling throne!"

And surely did the entourage soon cross the dim horizon,
Lumbering in greater pomp than ever man laid eyes on.
The horse guard mocked the beggar, laughing, prodding him with poles
And growled, "Begone, ye possum; yea, crawl back into yer holes!"

Then followed gaily colored wagons frought with flags and bowers
And ranks of lovely maidens casting petals, grapes, and flowers.
The carriages all reeked with smoke from braised and roasting meat,
A feast fit for the potentate, with which to fill his beak.

The beggar sat upon a stone, to catch his breath awhile,
Half crying and half laughing at the wretched scene so vile.
Anon, the Emperor's wagon came, with gold and purple wheels,
And who should stick his head out but that selfsame Chief of Heels!

He had a crown upon his head and beef betwixt his jowls;

The beggar thought it comical, which prompted him to howl!
When he espied the beggar man, the Emperor, enraged,
Stopped the whole procession from within his gilded cage!

The Emperor now quit his coach and bellowed, "Here is treason!"
And I shall see you bow before me now, or know the reason!"
The beggar rose up from the rock and stood upon the sod,
And said "I do not hate you, but I bow to none but God."

The captain of the cavalry came up and drew his sword,
Said "Let me take his head off, Sire! I hope for no reward."
"Nay, let him go, this old poltroon, the mis'rable sorry drool,
The dogs will make short work of him! Be off, ye scrowdy fool!"

And so with banners waving did the royal train proceed,
On the widely-taken road of worldly wisdom, vice, and greed.
The weary beggar plodded on the lesser traveled way,
To claim his sure Inheritance he knew would come one day.

Survival of the Fittest

Darwin lugged his sea-bag on the "Beagle" setting sails
Bound for the Galapagos to study frogs and snails.
Not content to rest upon the Genesis account,
He formulated theories and bandied them about.
"Life on earth evolved," he said, "and only strong survive."
So Man is not accountable to God, and he must strive.
His writings have become a seat on which the scholar sittest:
That life is merely dog-eat-dog, "Survival of the fittest."

And true enough, it seems to be, the strong replace the weak;
Society rejects a man who turns the other cheek.
We're born by forces unbeknownst, and then we live our days,
To bite and claw each other's flesh like rats caught in a maze.
And all their vain philosophies, the drivel that they spittest,
Is now encompassed by the phrase "Survival of the Fittest!"

But every time a rare bird dies, we hear the same ones shout,
Proclaiming we should try to save the weak ones dying out!
"Quickly, save the spotted owl!" through their teeth they grittest,
So they do not believe their code, "Survival of the Fittest."

And if monkeys came from tadpoles, why, then, tadpoles do we see?
If man evolved from monkeys, why then monkeys still there be?
Why are fish in water, and the birds soar in the skies?
If God created each one special, are we trusting lies?

Darwin's notion on the surface seems it's worth the time;
And sounds quite good to everyone who's fit and in their prime.
But should you fall and break your back and wind up in a bed,
Don't be surprised if suddenly the people want you dead!
If you outlive your usefulness, the mob will say to you,
"The fate that befalls animals is good for humans too!"
Be careful what you promulgate, the tangled web thou knittest:
Or one day they will stab you with "Survival of the fittest!"

The Cure

God knew me 'ere I was formed in Mother's inward part,
He saw my unborn body and beheld my beating heart.
And I looked forward to my birth when I would sing my song,
But one day something happened to me, when the world went wrong.

I was relaxing in the womb, and musing on my life,
When suddenly I was assaulted by a sterile knife!
I never saw the suction pump that took me out in stages,
And in a flash my soul was flung into the endless ages.

I am in Heaven now, because I had no chance to sin,
And I hold no hard feelings 'gainst the ones who did me in...
I would have liked to know my mom, and all the childhood joys
Of snow, and flowers, and swimming pools with other girls and boys...

But there's no use in shedding tears, for I am not in pain,
And I'll be here to greet you, if your faith is not in vain.
But if I had been left to live, I might have found the answer
For a car that runs on water, and a common cure for cancer.

Heal our Land

Lord, we're on a tightrope wire;
The price of gas is climbing higher,
We're beset by floods and fire;
Heal our land!

Enemies do us surround;
Vice and crime benights our town,
Truth is thrown unto the ground,
Heal our land!

Racial wars go on forever,
Ethnic folks can't get together,
Seems we're stuck in stormy weather;
Heal our land!

America's a house divided;
Laws and politics lopsided,
Crucial issues undecided,
Heal our land!

Murders, shootings on the rise,
Cheats are propagating lies,
Wolves are dressed in sheep disguise,
Heal our land!

People don't respect the preachers,
Movies tout demonic creatures,
Schoolboys now attack their teachers;
Heal our land!

Drivers rage in rotten mood;
Hungry children needing food;
None can tell the bad from good;
Heal our land!

Lord we need a mercy bath
To spare us from Almighty Wrath!
Save our souls, and light our path!
Heal our land!

The Great Gamble

Many gamble freely against odds that cannot pay,
They might as well just burn it up, or give it all away
To people that they do not know, who do not care a bit
Who lives, or dies, or walks the streets, or falls into a pit.

I've passed by their casinos in the dark at three AM,
And seen the cars jammed in those lots, the bumpers end-to-end.
And cried for souls who gave themselves to Fortune's beck and call,
Who bet their last dime on a pipe dream, and then lost it all.

But even anti-gamblers will sell everything they own,
If they are sure they'll win the jackpot when the dice are thrown!
I've found the grandest payoff that the world has ever heard,
And it's the ancient Gospel that is found in God's own Word.

The rules are very simple, and anyone can play…
You yield your sinful life to Christ, and win eternal day.
So if you rue your life imperfect, call on Jesus' Name,
And His shed blood will wash your soul, and you'll not be the same!

We do gamble, each of us, on what we think is true,
And cannot force the people to believe the things we do.
Let others do as they might wish, and follow whom they may,
But I have staked it all on Christ, the Life, the Truth, the Way.

If God Should Go on Strike

"He causes his sun to rise on the evil and the good, and sends rain on the righteous and the unrighteous."—Matthew 5:45

How good it is that God above has never gone on strike,
Because He was not treated fair, in things He didn't like.
If only He had given up and said, "That's it, I'm through!
I've had enough of those ingrates, so this is what I'll do:

"I'll give my 'pink slip' to the sun; cut off the heat supply!
And then I think I'll stop the rain, and drain the rivers dry.
Then I'll stifle heartbeats, and smother everyone
By turning off their oxygen 'till every breath is gone!"

You know He would be justified, if fairness was the game,
For no one has been more abused, nor met with more disdain
Than God, and yet he carries on, supplying you and me
With all the favors of His grace, and everything for free!

I think of how the Son of God did suffer such a loss,
Stooping down through time and space to die upon a cross.
How difficult it was for him to serve the Father's will,
Which, if he had refused to do, we'd lie in darkness still!

Men say they want a better deal; to picket lines they go.
But what's the deal we've given Him to whom all things we owe?
We can't imagine hell on earth, nor what it would be like,
But that's the fix we'd all be in, if God should go on strike!

What Am I Bid?

What am I bid for this Nazarene,
What am I bid for this slave?
He won't command much at auction, I fear,
This Jew who claims he can save!

What am I bid for his Virgin Birth,
In a stable, at the back of an inn?
Not a very royal beginning,
For a King who died for our sin.

What am I bid for his mercy,
The good that he did for the poor?
He's worth thirty pieces of silver, I guess…
Is anyone offering more?

What am I bid for his Gospel,
That captured so many hearts?
He spoke like no man before him, they say…
Who'll give me twenty to start?

What am I bid for his healings,
The balm for the sick and the lame?
He opened the eyes of blind Bartimaeus…
Come on, at least give me ten?!

What am I bid for his miracles?
He walked on the waves of the sea!
He even raised Lazarus up from the grave!
Who'll start the bidding at three?

What am I bid for his passion,
The beatings and thorns for a crown?
Nails in his hands and a slashin',
Who'll give me one penny down?

What am I bid for his empty tomb,
Proving he rose from the dead?
He ascended indeed into Heaven, they say…
From whence he will soon come again…!

I know he don't look like a bargain,
He's meek, and acquainted with grief.
But He is the Way, the Truth and the Life…
What is He worth to ya, chief?

Amnesty

They'd bombed the judge's house, and sent two governors to heaven,
And shot the marketplaces up with A-K forty sevens.
The rebels ducked the helicopters flying overhead,
Shooting off some rocket guns and show'ring them with lead.

Then the rebels slid into their jungle hideaway,
Laughing at the army, which pursued them day to day.
And as they sat beside the campfire in a circle round,
The helicopter dropped some leaflets, covering the ground.

They said, "If any rebel, who is fighting us today,
Will merely drop his weapon at the outpost miles away,
And sign an oath of loyalty, and promise not to run,
That he will be forgiven any wrong that he has done."

"The army does not care how long you've fought against our arms,
It matters not how many you have killed, whatever harm,
If you will just surrender to us, we will clear the slate…
You have 'till noon tomorrow; after that, 'twill be too late!"

"The pigs must think we're stupid," the rebel leader said,
"They wait for us to show ourselves, and then cut off our heads."
Thusly did the rebels spurn the offer from on high,
But one young man named Rico sat and pondered with a sigh…

"I've been a lonely rebel now for almost seven years,

We gave our homeland nothing except terror, death and fears.
What do I have to lose if I accept this amnesty?
If I stay here, I'll be dead, the same as if I flee."

Rico left the camp that night while others were asleep,
And made his way toward Outpost Uno in the darkness deep.
The guardsmen called a halt to him, but looked a mite perplexed…
As Rico tossed his weapon down and wondered what was next.

They took him to a concrete shack by military car,
And led him to the commandante, smoking a cigar.
"I heard about an amnesty," said Rico with a tear,
"I want to see my family and kiss my loved ones dear.
Once I sought adventure fighting with the rebel band,
But now I rue my life of crime, and swear with lifted hand…
Tho' I am guilty as the devil, if you set me free,
I will pay taxes, love my country, and serve loyally."

The commandante leaned aback, and took a puff of smoke,
Propped up his feet and thought awhile, and gave his beard a stroke,
At last he reached into his desk and took out pen and ink,
And showed the paper's dotted line: "You sign here, I think."

Rico left that concrete shack expecting to be shot,
The army kept their promise to him, therefore he was not.
He ran and leaped like baby calves released from yonder stall,
Raised a family, went to work, and found new life withal.

God shows amnesty to sinners in the selfsame way,
If you will come before the Cross and swear God to obey,
And lay your weapons all aside with which you fought so free,
It will not matter what your crimes: forgiven you shall be.

Seven hours later did the amnesty expire,
And helicopter gunships rained down sulfur, lead, and fire
Upon the sleepy rebel band, and they did not escape.
They waited just a bit too long the amnesty to take.

Why Pray When You Can Worry?

"Cast all your anxiety on him because he cares for you." I Peter 5:7

Why pray when you can worry,
And give yourself a pain?
Why rest when you can hurry
And scurry around in vain?
Why give the matter to Him
When you can fret and moan?
Why trust, when you can make believe
The battle is your own?

For are we not all self-made men, who cover every base?
So why consult the Maker, He who flung the stars in space?
And since we have the answers to all life's mysteries,
Why waste our time in worship? Why get upon our knees...?

Why pray when we lack wisdom, and we don't know what to do?
How can the Master help us, who has all Time in view?
When gold and silver leave us, and we cry about our ills,
Why ask the Owner of the cattle on a thousand hills?

Why ASK when you can argue,
And stress yourself with doubt?
Why SEEK when you can mutter
"Guess I'll never find it out."
Why KNOCK at Heaven's portals

Instead of sweat and stew?
Why pray when you can worry...
Like it all depends on you?

Me, Myself, and I

Three sinners lurk upon the earth with hearts as hard as stone;
If only we could turn their hearts toward Heaven's royal throne.
Oh, for Grace, that they may be persuaded from on high!
For these three culprits bear the names of Me, Myself, and I.

It's not the Whore of Babylon that's causing all the grief;
It's not the village drunkard who is of all sinners chief,
But these three characters, debauched, who make the angels cry:
Those dirty scoundrels by the names of Me, Myself and I.

They, mocking, stood at Calvary, when Christ hung on the tree,
They drove the nails into his hands and spikes into his feet.
They thrust the spear into his side, and caused the Lamb to die.
Did any man do God more harm than Me, Myself, and I?

Yet these charmers seem to have good names within the town;
They go to church each Sunday morn, and sing a joyful sound.
They sit right up attentive, even wear the coat and tie!
God only knows how cold the hearts of Me, Myself and I!

How few the times they've knelt in prayer, or persevered in faith;
How few the souls that they have led toward Heaven's pearly gates.
I fear they are not ready for that meeting in the sky!
And Oh! I fear the reckoning for Me, Myself and I!

If ever were benighted blokes in desperate need of prayer,
It's these three aimless drifters who live without a care.
To them has much been given, therefore much will be required...
Oh, Lord, I beg thee, save the souls of Me, Myself and I!

My Honest Prayer

Bless me Lord, bless me, with leisure and ease!
Keep me from trouble and death and disease;
Give me more money than I ever can spend,
So I don't have to budget, or borrow… or lend…
And a house far away from the poor peoples' place,
And freedom from guilt when I harden my face.
In short, Lord, please bless me, so I can be free…
…from the person you're trying to get me to be!

The Mustard Seed

Mark 4:30-32

Jesus was hungry and looked for figs upon the branch of a tree.
Finding none, he cursed the plant and it dried up immediately.
His disciples stared in disbelief, asking "How can this thing be?"
And Jesus told them all you need is the faith of a mustard seed.

Jesus came to Cana town, to share a wedding feast.
The harried host ran out of juice; ashamed, to say the least.
When Jesus overheard the plight, he straightway took the lead,
And turned plain water into wine, with the faith of a mustard seed!

Jairus was a Jewish ruler known throughout the land;
He lost his daughter to the Reaper, and sadly held her hand.
He said to Jesus, "If you can, restore her life I plead!"
Jesus raised her from the dead with the faith of a mustard seed!

Tired and starving were the thousands following Him that day,
They could not feed that many mouths with even eight month's pay!
A young man brought some loaves and fishes, all he had, indeed…
But Jesus fed the entire crowd by the faith of a mustard seed.

Mary and Martha were bereaved; the Lord was occupied.
They chided, "Lord, if you'd been here, our brother'd not have died!"
"I am the Resurrection, Mary, my words you must heed!"
And Lazarus came forth from the grave by the faith of a mustard seed!

The Kingdom's like that seed of mustard, planted in a field.
Although it seems the smallest thing, it gives the greatest yield.
If you've been asking "What is truth? And how much do I need?"
Believe on Christ with a little faith... the size of a mustard seed!

The Lost Coin

"In the same way, I tell you, there is rejoicing in the presence of the angels of God over one sinner who repents."
—Luke 15:10

She counted out her silver coins
To ascertain all ten were there;
Alas! She counted only nine…
One was missing; where?

The first thing was to light a lamp
So she could see with undimmed eye;
And so we too must have a light,
The Word of God Most High.

The next course was to sweep the house
To get out all the dirt and grime;
As we must also rid our lives
Of every sin and crime.

Then she began to search the floor
In every hidden nook and cranny;
As we must also seek the lost
In every home and shanty.

In a corner dank and dusky
Shone that silver brightly shining.

Twas the missing coin! Hurray!
What joy there is in finding!

Thus does Jesus seek lost sheep
From every tribe and tongue and nation,
When he finds one, all the angels
Cheer in CELEBRATION!

If I Only Had a Hundred

"Lord, if I had a hundred dollars,
With Ben Franklin's picture on the front,
I could barely pay the rent, Then alas it would be spent…
Is that really all that I would want?

"Lord, let me raise it to five hundred,
That would really give my face a shine.
I could buy a suit of clothes, But that's all, and so it goes…
A thousand would be maybe more in line.

"Lord, if I asked you for two thousand,
That is what I'm really praying for.
It won't get me very far… It won't even buy a car!
Hold on now, let me think some more.

"Lord, if you'd give me seven thousand
I could get a nice used car and then be done.
But what if it breaks down While I'm in some rural town?
I'd be broke and could not get back home…

"Lord, let me make it twenty thousand,
Just to cover extras, frills, and such
I don't want to be too greedy, But I wish to not be needy…
I'm wondering if fifty is too much…

"Lord, with a hundred thousand dollars,
That would end the question and be finished.
I could buy a residence, But, in using common sense,
I would not want that stash to be diminished…

"Lord, if I only had a million!
More and more folks have that much today…
I could live off interest, But after taxes there'd be less…
Hmmm! I really need two million put away…"

Hours later, I was up to near a billion
With country real estate, yacht, and a crew.
Then I came back to my senses, And forgot all my expenses.
"Lord, how much should I be giving you?"

The Broken Starter

On a Caribbean Island, my rusty small sedan
I found would stop quite readily, but would not start again!
I spent an entire morning with my head beneath the hood,
Sweating, fussing, guessing what was bad, and what was good.

I pushed the ailing heap to a mechanic down the road
(Reasoning that this would be more cheap than being towed).
He knew me not from Adam, but he said with toothy grin,
"Just leave it where it sits, man, and I'll try to fit you in."

He could tell I had misgivings, and he tried to reassure,
"If your car is sick, man, I am going to find the cure.
But there really is one question you must answer in your head,
And that is 'Do you trust me?' Or I might as well be dead."

I left the car behind me and walked homeward in the rain,
Wondering if I would ever see that thing again!
Would that stranger soak me? Was I being very wise?
Did he see the Yankee dollar shining brightly with his eyes?

At sundown I returned to find the car as good as new;
The fellow solved the problem just by tightening a screw!
With gritted teeth, I asked him if the bill was very large,
He handed me the keys and said "For trusting me, no charge!"

How mighty like the Gospel, when for mercy we implore,
And our rusty soul needs fixing, helpful love, and so much more...
We owe a debt we cannot pay, are blind and cannot see...
But when Jesus sees we trust Him, He does the work for free!

The Lighthouse and the Battleship

The keeper climbed the lighthouse stairs before the fall of night;
The giant lantern creaked and groaned and cast a ray of light,
Beaming forth a warning to be heeded far and wide
By any would-be mariner across the foaming tide.

The lighthouse had been built of yore upon the coastal rocks.
But now there came a battleship, making thirty knots!
The captain on the bridge could see the glimmer and the glow;
He thought he had the right-of-way, and grabbed his radio.

"This is the battleship, you hear?" the Captain said with pride.
"We're on a vital mission here, so you must turn aside."
The lighthouse keeper answered back, "Sir you don't comprehend!
It's *you* who has to alter course, and very soon, my friend!"

The Captain snapped a curt reply, "We're got no time to lose!
Don't argue with the navy, buster! Get your carcass moved!"
"I don't know who you think you are," the keeper did rebound,
"But we don't move for vessels, it's the other way around."

Now enraged, the Captain had the guns trained on the light,
And was ready, aimed to fire, when the rocks came into sight!
He ordered "hard to starboard!" And the ship lurched off the line
And narrowly avoided that disaster just in time.

Oh, we may think we're sailing in the sharpest thing afloat,
But the Gospel is the Lighthouse, and you and I the boat!

He Chose Me

"Blessed are those you choose and bring near to live in your courts!"—Psalm 65:4

The Bible says God chose me from the birthplace of the world,
That I might believe his Son and from the grave be hurled.
Chosen, like some Studebaker in a junkyard lot;
Chosen, though the paint was peeling and the engine shot;
I guess he knew I could be fixed to run eternally,
And I'm so glad that He chose me!

The Bible says God knew believers through the ages past,
That from eternity gone by he met our needs at last.
Chosen, like some orphaned urchin taken from the street;
Chosen, tho' my manners rough, and sneakers on my feet;
He took me in and dressed me up in robes of royalty,
And I'm so glad that He chose me!

The Bible says the Lamb was slain before the world began,
Christ died for sinners, rose again, and all within God's plan.
And I feel chosen, like a building set to be torn down…
Chosen, though the rooms were dirty and the windows brown,
I guess he knew that all I needed was His T.L.C.,
And I'm so glad that He chose me!

Trust You

I fall upon my face Asking simply for the grace
To trust you.

If the sun does not give light, I'm going to do what's right
And trust you.

If my friends all walk away, I'll be here all day,
And trust you.

If the highway turns to gravel, I'll follow where you travel
And trust you.

Though it ruins all my fun, If it costs me all I own,
I trust you.

So if I have to cry, Even if I have to die...
I trust you.

When People Pray

Friends and loved ones that we know
Are lost in sin and sinking low;
Darkness hides their light of day,
But something happens when people pray.

Pastors strain with heavy loads,
Carnal saints have far to go.
We can help them along their way,
For something happens when people pray.

Many hold to strange beliefs;
Missionaries cross the reefs;
Oft they know not what to say...
But something happens when people pray.

Churches are asking "Where are the youth?"
Neighbors are asking, "What is the truth?"
Many wander far astray,
But something happens when people pray.

Sick depression blights our souls;
Wolves are plotting to ravage the fold;
But we can blow the clouds away,
For something happens when people pray!

My Bubble Balloon

I live in a bubble balloon,
Which seals me like a cocoon
From the cares of the day which might cause me dismay;
I love my bubble balloon.

Inside my bubble balloon,
My song is a happy tune!
No woes to hound me; just rosy hues 'round me
Here in my bubble balloon.

Inside my bubble balloon
I live in my own little womb.
I choose what I want, and my wild desires flaunt,
Here in my bubble balloon.

For here in my bubble balloon
I can fly as high as the moon…
Be a king in a tower; anything's in my power
Inside my bubble balloon!

From outside my bubble balloon,
I hear them call, "Come to Christ soon!
You have to believe, and His cleansing receive…
You'll die in that bubble balloon!"

But here in my bubble balloon
I heed no such voice of doom.
Nobody can teach me, nobody can reach me,
Inside my bubble balloon.

The sands of time, like a dune,
Blow over my bubble balloon...
And the voices of warning grow dimmer each morning,
Inside my bubble balloon.

Alas, my bubble balloon
Is at last by the Judgment consumed!
And too late in the night, I find they were right;
Inside my... < POP! >

The Preacher

I stumbled, aimless, on one cloudy Sunday afternoon,
Shuffling on the sidewalk like a failure and buffoon.
My sermon about gossip caused a row in church that morn.
It offended Mrs. Cluckinghen; I wished I'd not been born.

I sat upon a bench to sob, tears plastering my face,
And planned a resignation letter, ending my disgrace.
When who should sit beside me but a white-haired man with cane,
Who gave me this advice before I asked him for his name.

"I used to pastor over there, that church with ivy vines…
I've cried upon this very bench since then, and many times.
It took me far too long to see, but you must learn it well:
Ice-cream-candy preaching doesn't rescue men from hell!

"I thought I'd win the wayward souls by mincing all my words,
Eliminating 'hell' and 'sin', which seemed to frazzle nerves.
I thought t'was being spiritual, but seems I was mistaken;
Now in my dreams, I hear the screams of friends the devil's taken!

"This vile world's no friend to Grace, to help us shun the wrong.
Don't feed the Lord's flock gingerbread, but preach the Gospel strong!
The preacher mustn't pussyfoot, or tickle sinners' ears.
'Woe when all speak well of thee,' so don't expect their cheers.

"Warn that vile adulterer, and pull the drunkard's hair!
Expose the greedy charlatan, lay false religion bare!
Don't let that gossip's tongue keep spreading wormwood's poison gall!
Attack that root of bitterness with sharpened axe and maul!

"You're bound to step on toes, my friend; expect your friends to scowl.
The stronger be the medicine, the more they're gonna howl!
We mustn't take it *personal* when sinners yell in pain…
You have to spank 'em, preacher boy! Don't give 'em Novocain!

"Once they're safe in Heaven with the alabaster beams,
And meet the One who died for them, and feed by sparkling streams,
They'll kiss your feet in gratitude for wounding but their pride,
Restraining them from evil, when you could have run to hide."

I told my saintly comforter, "My pity party's done.
I fresh resolve to fight for souls until the battle's won."
I dried my eyes, and blew my nose, and then I combed my hair,
And turned again to shake his hand… but there was no one there!

The Fireman

A fireman, driving past apartments, saw a puff of smoke within,
He skidded to a stop, and, on his cellphone, called it in.
Then he banged upon the walls to warn the people in that place,
"Fire! Fire! Your house is burning! Everyone must leave in haste!"

Cooby Dooper's eyelids opened, as he lolled upon his bed;
"Who's that making such a hooplah? Knock that fellow on the head!"
"Call the cops," said Diddle Piddle, throwing shoes across the room.
"The hateful beast, disturbing people trying to sleep in 'till noon!"

Then the fireman went and got his fire hatchet from his car,
Yelling out alarms and warnings, he commenced to break the door.
Smoozie Sweetz was watching soaps, and heard the noise out on the lawn;
"How am I to watch TV with all that racket going on?"

Darnold Bleezer scratched his armpit, went and poured a shot of wine,
Maizie Moocher donned her bathrobe, cracked the door a hair and whined:
"A crazy loon with bulging eyes is running loose out in the hall!
He hates us; he berates us, and he's got an axe! He'll kill us all!"

Soon the smoke had billowed so the fireman could no longer breathe,
But he hoped to rescue someone, so he dropped down to his knees.
"Please God, make them smell the smoke! Please God can you make them see?
Can't they recognize their peril? Don't they know that they must flee?"

Just then, flames broke through the roof; a crashing timber knocked him down.
The people still remained aloof, believing they were safe and sound.
Once more he bawled urgently, "Get out! Get out! You've one last chance!"
But everyone insulted him, and heckled him with raves and rants.

Suddenly the flames burst forth and trapped the denizens inside.
They all burned in the inferno, they could not be reached in time.
The trucks arrived, as our lone fireman cried aloud in racking sobs,
"Why can't people simply heed alarms and warnings sent from God?"

Come When Called

In the years of my childhood, when supper was served,
My mother would call with a shout,
And I was to drop my whatevers and come,
Or I would just go without.

Once when the voice of my mom did resound,
The playmates said to me, "Hey!
You won't be too late! Your supper will wait!"
And thus I was coaxed to delay.

But when I arrived, I learned to my grief
That my plate contained nothing at all.
And I pitifully cried, but my mother would chide,
"Next time, you come when called."

Once in each life, or maybe twice,
God's Spirit speaks to a man,
Explaining that he is in need of Christ,
Showing him Salvation's plan.

The doubters will try to throw him off track
Or lure him with silver and gold,
Saying, "Don't be a fool, you have to be cool!
Don't think about God 'til you're old!"

But you must not wait! Press on toward the Gate
To enter God's banqueting hall!
He died for you, sinner, but you may miss your dinner
If you do not come when called!

Two Little Juveniles

Two little juveniles, sitting in the school:
Aughtey was well-behaved, Naughty broke the rules.
The teacher was puzzled why the one did not do right…
But the answer lay in what the two were doing late at night!

Aughtey read from Genesis, to know where he was from,
Naughty read the books that taught he came from primal scum.
Aughtey read the Pentateuch, to know what saith the Scroll,
Naughty clicked on porno sites which caused his eyes to roll.
Aughtey read of Kings who were punished when they strayed,
Naughty wasted money in the video arcade.
Aughtey read Ezra, and learned revival's plan;
Naughty watched the poker shows, to be a gambling man.
Aughtey read Job, and learned of patience under stress;
Naughty threw a tantrum if he wasn't always blessed.
Aughtey studied Psalms, and found comfort when in doubt;
Naughty studied nothing, and his grades have found him out!
Aughtey read the Proverbs, and he learned to be discreet;
Naughty got his wisdom from delinquents on the street.
Aughtey learned from Daniel, who always paused to pray,
Naughty learned the swear words, and practiced every day.
The Gospels Aughtey studied, as he sought the Christ of old…
Naughty chewed and swallowed any lie that he was told.
In the book of Acts, Aughtey read of Holy Spirit fire;
While Naughty sought from Hollywood the fleshly muck and mire.

From Romans, Aughtey learned to fear and flee the wage of sin,
But Naughty, reading books on witchcraft, vowed to plunge right in.
Aughtey learned from Corinthians to love with charity,
While Naughty learned to back-talk from the sitcoms on TV.
Aughtey read Galatians, how Christ fulfils our needs,
And in Ephesians learned we're saved by grace, and not by deeds!
Philippians taught the young lad of Christlike servanthood,
And how to train his mind to only think about the good.
Thessalonians gave him hope, to think one day he'll fly…
And Paul urged him, thru Timothy, "press onward toward the prize!"
The book of Hebrews gave him stock to root his faith upon;
Plus letters by those sure disciples, Peter, James, and John,
Who from prison and from Patmos wrote of mighty things to come:
The doom of sinners, song of saints, and earthly trials done!
By this the young man's faith was given wings and hands and feet,
To live out his salvation with behavior fit and meet.
Small wonder that such inspiration made him want to spend
His life on slightly higher ground than his silly little friend.
Yes, two little juveniles, sitting in the school:
Aughtey studied the Word of God. Naughty was a fool.

Bethlehem Carol

Truly did Isaiah say, "All we like sheep have gone astray;"
But at Bethlehem, the angels sang as God professed his love to Man.

The Lad grew up to heal and feed the crowds who came to him in need.
And all the people did he teach, for "No man spoke with words like these!"
But lo, some schemers soon assayed to have the Son of God betrayed;
They had him nailed upon a cross: Sinner's gain, and devil's loss!
Once Man was humbled under Law; now God's Grace is free to all.
The precious blood of the Lord of Hosts supplants the gore of bulls and goats.
Once worshipers, with unclean hands, didst mourn the veil 'twixt God and Man.
But by his death, the Holy One did rend that curtain, once and done!
So now, all peoples who believe, "No condemnation" shall receive;
The Son of God was pierced and torn; thus He our punishment hath borne…
…And, three days later, rose again… as seen by some five hundred men…
before ascending out of sight. But he'll return, to set things right!

So those who await Messiah still must needs look back; for God hath will'd
to show precisely who's to reign: It's Jesus Christ we now proclaim!

He Was Made King, However

"His subjects hated him and sent a delegation after him to say, 'We don't want this man to be our king.' 15
"He was made king, however."—*Luke 19:14*

There is no other name from Heaven given unto man,
None by which we must be saved, and experience God's plan.
For God has sent his Only Son to be the Only Savior,
And though the rebels stamp their feet, "He was made King, however."

Satan sidled up to Jesus, tempting him to sin.
But Christ rebuffed him every time, and never would give in.
Thusly did the Prince of Darkness fail in his endeavor,
He tried to conquer Jesus Christ who "was made King, however!"

Jesus healed the sick and lame, and spoke like none e'er spoke;
He raised the dead and fed the thousands with the fish and loaves.
Judas tried to sell him out for thirty coins of silver.
If only they could see him now! "He was made King, however!"

The kings of earth all take their stand against the Glorious Son:
"Let us break these chains asunder! Join hands, everyone!"
The One enthroned in heaven laughs; "They think they are so clever!"
And 'twill be said of Jesus soon, "He was made King however!"

The world beholds believers now with pity and their scorn,
Mockers do deny the Truth; this world their sole reward.
They somehow think that they will win, that they will suffer never;
But too late, they will cry, "Alas! He was made King, however!"

One day every knee shall bow, and every tongue confess
That Jesus Christ is Lord of all, and God forever blessed.
Now Jesus keeps His faithful ones with love no pow'r can sever,
So we can sing in perfect joy, "He was made King however!"

Damaged Goods

We do not buy a house or car without a close inspection,
We nitpick every corner and examine every section.
And we don't sign the deal unless we are convinced we should,
And never will we ever pay for damaged goods!

There was a woman at the Well,
Lost and on her way to hell;
Tossed from man to man who lusted,
But Jesus saved her when she trusted.

Another girl was caught in the act
Of adultery; a proven fact!
Christ did not condemn the whore,
But simply told her "sin no more."

Zacchaeus got rich collecting tax,
But he gave all that money back
When Jesus asked himself to dinner!
He sought, and taught, and saved that sinner.

Saul of Tarsus, so refined,
For "The Way" he had no time.
Chased believers town to town,
But the Hound of Heaven tracked him down.

The Bible's full of damaged people
Redeemed from the realms of evil.
Harlots, cowards, loudmouths, thieves,
Many scoundrels were retrieved…

But it's not cheap to break those chains;
It costs pure blood from sinless veins!
Only Christ could qualify
To purchase us to live on high.

And He'll buy nearly anyone! No picky shopper He,
And this is how I know it's true: He paid top price for me.

Ask, Seek, Knock

Matthew 7:7

Ask ye prayers of many types,
Requests, all shapes and sizes;
When it pleases God to bless,
He'll add no bane besides.

Seek Him, wise men from afar,
And search His sacred Book;
To thee the truth shall be reveal'd,
If earnestly ye look.

So keep a-knockin' at His door,
And on his Gate be bangin';
He will arise and answer thee;
He will not leave ye hangin'!

Prayers

Long prayers, short prayers, prayers of all sizes
Prayers when the sun sets and again when it rises.
Prayers on our knees or standing or sitting.
Prayers at the workbench or doing our knitting.
Prayers when we travel and prayers when we stay.
Prayers when we work and prayers when we play.
Prayers of thanksgiving and prayers for our nation
Prayers of confession and strong supplication.
Prayers giving praise and prayers in our song,
Prayers when we wake, and prayers all the day long.

Go to Church When It's Raining

Go to church when it's raining
And the mud sticks to your feet,
If we gather together in only fair weather,
How will the devil be beat?

Go to church when you're hurting,
Visit His house when you're low;
Disciple yourself not only in wealth,
But worship Him also in woe.

Go to church when you've failed him,
And your shamefulness tempts you to hide.
If we pretend we are always victorious,
Is it not spiritual pride?

Go to church when they hate you,
And snub you without reason,
For if you attend with only your friends,
"What do ye more than the heathen?"

Go to the church when it's boring,
And the service has lost all its zest;
Make it your call to infuse life to all!
Bless others, and you shall be blest!

The Greatest Winners

When someone saves an Orca Whale or wins the Nobel Prize,
The world applauds with clapping hands and praise mounts to the skies.
Or if he scores the touchdown to win the greatest game,
The newsmen vie for interviews; there's no end to his fame.

The world's great movie magnates hold award festivities,
Rich nabobs courting smiles and handshakes from celebrities
Who live in marble palaces like emperors of Rome,
And neither you, nor paparazzi, can get near their home.

True missionaries labor long with worn and weary hands,
To bring the Gospel to a tribe in some far distant land,
Or mop the restroom floor at church, or hand out Bread to sinners…
I wonder who, on that Last Day, will be the greatest winners?

The Erythraean Sibyl

(Adapted from a poem mentioned in St. Augustine's "City of God")

The Roman Historian Varro declares there were many "sibyls" (sort of like prophets) like the sibyl of Erythrae, who lived in the time of the Trojan War (1200 BC). He wrote some things concerning the Christ, who of course had not appeared as of yet. This shows that ancient peoples far from Israel had an understanding of the concept of a coming Messiah. In the Christmas story, the Magi came a thousand miles from Persia to Jerusalem to seek "he that is born King of the Jews." Would they have done that if they had nothing more substantial to go on than a strange star in the heavens? No, they knew the prophecies about Messiah and energetically set out to seek him. Wise men today still seek the Lord while he may be found!
Behold the insight of this philosopher! I have altered some verses only to make them rhyme, but did not change the meaning, and most of the following words are from this sibyl of Erythrae, twelve hundred years before Christ!

"Judgment shall moisten the earth with water and blood,
Ever enduring, behold! The King shall come!
Sent first in flesh, yet Judge at the last of the world;
That God, whom believing and faithless alike shall behold.
Uplifted with saints, when at last the ages are ended.
Seated before Him are souls with every knee bended.
Rejected now are the idols and long hidden treasure;
Earth is consumed by the fire, and it burns without measure.

Each one shall publish those actions he did in the dark;
Secrets of every man's heart the Lord God shall mark.
Then shall be weeping and wailing, yea, gnashing of teeth;
Eclipsed is the sun and moon, darkness on earth beneath.
Exalted by Him are the valleys, while the mountains are lowered.
Utterly gone among men are the vile and the froward.
Oh, what an end he makes! All the earth broken in shivers;
Swelling together at once are the flames and the rivers!
Then the archangel's trump shall resound from the skies,
Over the wicked, who groan, having trusted in lies.
Trembling, the earth shall be opened, revealing its fire
Rivers of brimstone shall fall upon all like a pyre.
Saints, in their body and soul, light and life shall inherit:
But those who are guilty shall burn in the brimstone they merit."

The Cross of Bronze

"Just as Moses lifted up the snake in the desert, so the Son of Man must be lifted up, that everyone who believes in him may have eternal life."—John 3:14, 15

Long time ago in the wilderness,
The Israelites were put to the test;
They grumbled and whined, and made their God so mad.
So He sent serpents to bite their toes
And chasten them with a rod of woes,
But they cried out "God forgive us!" And He said:

"Make thee a pole in the shape of a cross
And on it hang a serpent of bronze;
The form of the very snake that troubles thee.
And you who are bitten, before you die,
Just look on that form which is hanging high."
And those who beheld that cross healed instantly!

Time has passed, but not the curse;
We're not getting better, but waxing worse.
We're bitten by sin, and are on our way to hell.
But God so loved us from the edge of time,
That He sent us His Son to bleed and die,
And rise from the grave so that we might be made well.

"Make thou a rugged cross of wood

And on it hang the One so good…
Who became the form of the sin that troubles thee.
And ye who are guilty, before you die,
Just think on that form which hung so high
Yet rose from the dead! Behold Him… and be free!"

Yes, think on the cross on which He swayed,
And think on His blood… your ransom paid…
And say with your lips: "Lord Jesus, I believe."

Light at the End

There is light at the end of the tunnel,
There is hope for the people of faith;
There is rest for the weary believer,
On the Day that we see Jesus' face!

He is coming with all tender mercies
To teach us to sing a new song;
He will solve all our church controversies,
As we see all the things we had wrong.

No more shall we sanctify preference,
Nor squabble o'er forms of our praise;
Not a soul will be proud in His presence,
We'll be stunned by the fact that we're saved.

There's a wonderful reckoning coming,
When the Lord makes an end of the fray;
He'll reward us for faithfully running,
And crush the old serpent one day.

Yea, soon the veil shall be lifted,
No more shall we struggle with sin,
No more by the de'il to be sifted,
When the Lord's Golden Age enters in!

Well Done!

Jesus came to save us from the penalty of sin,
And make us fit for Heaven so that we could enter in.
But while the sun keeps rising, we've got a job to do,
Will we hear the Master say when time on Earth is through?

Well done! Well done!
Good and loyal were you, faithful, tried and true!
The fight of faith is over, the victory is won,
Well done, my children, well done!

Jesus loves the Father, the Father loves the Son,
And they will never leave us, until the race is run.
He promises to answer if only we will pray,
But will the Lord find faith upon the Earth until that Day?

Well done! Well done!
Good and faithful were you, believers tried and true!
The fight you fought is over, the victory is won,
Well done, my children, well done!

No man knows the hour when Jesus shall return,
And gives to all the harvesters rewards that they have earned.
But we must occupy the fields until that glorious day.
Can you see him smile, my friend? And can you hear him say…?

Well done! Well done!
Good and faithful were you, believers tried and true!
The fight you fought is over, the victory is won,
Well done, my children, well done!

Psalm 107

"Give thanks to the LORD for his unfailing love, for his love endures forever."

Some wandered lonely in desert waste,
Finding no city to call their place.
Hungry and thirsty, and their lives ebbed away,
But they cried to the LORD and he heard them say…

"Give thanks to the LORD for his unfailing love,
Give thanks to the LORD for his unfailing love,
Water for the thirsty, and food for our soul,
His love will endure forever, I know!"

Some sat in darkness and deepest gloom,
Prisoners under the sentence of doom.
But when they cried to the LORD from their cell,
He saved them out of the deepest hell.

"Give thanks to the LORD for his unfailing love,
Give thanks to the LORD for his unfailing love,
Water for the thirsty, and food for our soul,
His love will endure forever, I know!"

Some became fools through rebellious ways,
And suffered affliction because they strayed.
But they called to Jesus from the gates of death,

And He saved them out of their deep distress!

"Give thanks to the LORD for his unfailing love,
Give thanks to the LORD for his unfailing love,
Water for the thirsty, and food for our soul,
His love will endure forever, I know!"

Others went out on the sea in ships;
Storms almost brought them down to the depths;
But they cried out to God from the reeling decks,
And he led them into the Haven of Rest!

"Give thanks to the LORD for his unfailing love,
Give thanks to the LORD for his unfailing love,
Water for the thirsty, and food for our soul,
His love will endure forever, I know!"

Are We There Yet?

Aren't we just like children in the back seat of our van,
Riding with our Father across the weary land?
And we get so impatient while we're carryin' our load…
So we often cry to Daddy as we travel down the road,

Are we there yet? No! Are we there yet? No!
But we will be very soon!
Are we there yet? No! Are we there yet? No!
But one morning, night or noon,
Jesus will come in glory,
So tell the Old Old Story!
Are we there yet? No, not yet,
But we're on our way!

Travelin' down the highways and the byways with Him,
We often have a breakdown when things look pretty grim,
Fifteen miles from nowhere, the people pass us by,
We moan and groan to Heaven, just like the children cry:

Are we there yet? No! Are we there yet? No!
But we will be very soon!
Are we there yet? No! Are we there yet? No!
But one morning, night or noon,
Jesus will come in glory,
So tell the Old Old Story!

Are we there yet? No, not yet,
But any day!

Then we have a snowstorm and the wipers will not go,
Everything gets blurry and we have to travel slow,
The minutes turn to hours, with no motel in sight...
Hear the children cry out in the darkness of the night...

Are we there yet? No! Are we there yet? No!
But we will be very soon!
Are we there yet? No! Are we there yet? No!
But one morning, night or noon,
Jesus will come in glory,
So tell the Old Old Story!
Are we there yet? No, not yet, But any day!

Who Knows What God May Do

Is it hard to get up mornings
Are your sinews growing slack?
Does the road stretch long before you,
Do you feel like turning back?

Refrain: Who knows what God may do;
If we only ask him to?
And though he doesn't have to,
He gives grace to see us through…
Who knows what God may do?

Jesus said to ask believing,
Kneeling at His feet;
E'er long we'll be receiving
That our joy may be complete!

Oftentimes we get discouraged,
And our feet begin to slide,
But God can shower you with blessing,
That, and more beside!

We're beset with many rivals,
Seems the nation's torn in two!
But the fires of revival
Will be lit, if we pray through!

Don't give up before deliv'rance;
Can't you hear the horses' hooves?
Don't quit praying fifteen minutes
Before the mountain moves!

Refrain: Who knows what God may do;
If we only ask him to?
And though he doesn't have to,
He gives grace to see us through...
Who knows what God may do?

Babes in the Woods

Two babes held their father's hand as through the leas they trod,
Happy, singing melodies, picking flow'rs and pods.
Anon they entered dusky woods; the tykes to father flung,
Believing all was well, as long as to his arms they clung.

Th'Almighty tests the hearts of men to see where fealties lie,
And he may leave us in the woods, to hear to whom we sigh.
So children, fear not hoots of owls nor dread the fangs of beasts,
For God shall break the teeth of them and make of them his feasts.

Whenever ill times fall on us, whomever they may bind,
Wheree'er the foul clouds shadow thee, God's silver edge doth shine.
So children, when you look about you, keep on doing good,
And do not fear; He is quite near you, even in the woods.

A Still Small Voice

"And after the earthquake a fire; but the LORD was not in the fire:
and after the fire a still small voice."
—I Kings 19:12 KJV

Elijah heard the earthquake when the rocks came crashing down,
Ground a-shaking, mountains quaking, firestorms around.
But when the blustering had ceased, and all the smoke had cleared,
Elijah heard the "Still Small Voice," calming all his fears.

Do you still speak in a Still Small Voice, your wonders to display?
Do you still work your miracles in quiet hearts today?
Do you still whisper patiently with guidance firm and true?
Do you still speak in a Still Small Voice? I'm listening for you!

Samuel was a little tyke, dressed in a priestly robe,
Serving Eli at the Temple, only six years old.
He heard a voice call out his name, though gloomy was the hour,
He asked the Lord to speak to him; and God came down in power!

Do you still speak with a Still Small Voice when we incline our hearts?
Do you reveal great plans to us, or give us brand new starts?
You've been talking to your people since the ancient years,
So I pray as Samuel did: "Speak, Lord, your servant hears."

Hagar staggered with her son, rejected from the land...
Sun like hot brass o'er their heads, across the burning sand.

She hid the boy beneath a scrag, so not to see him die...
And then the Lord spoke peace to her, with words that saved their lives.

Do you still speak in a Still Small Voice, your comfort to impart?
Do you still offer solace to those with heavy hearts?
Do you still see the widow's and the single parent's tears?
Do you still speak in a Still Small Voice to those who perk their ears?

A eunuch rode his chariot, while reading from the prophet,
But could not make much sense of it, nor get the meaning off it.
But God sent Philip running with the proper explanation,
And from the Spirit's Still Small Voice, that eunuch got salvation!

Do you still speak in a Still Small Voice to people far and near?
Do you still call evangelists to preach the Word so clear?
Do you still awaken Philip, sending him with speed?
Do you still speak in a Still Small Voice, to meet Man's deepest need?

I O U

I owe a bill I cannot pay, and this is very true;
So I have written out to God my humble "I O U."

The "I" means **Inconvenience**, which often comes on me
When asked to do some Christian act of love or charity,
Or visit some poor sinner, or someone very old,
Or attend a deacons meeting driving through the snow and cold.
Or helping stranded motorists and coming home to find
The fam'ly went to dinner out, and I'd been left behind.
But oh, what does it matter? For in my soul I'm free,
And it wasn't too convenient when Jesus died for me.

The "O" stands for **Offenses** that must come from day to day:
The mocking scorn of pagans who make fun of those who pray,
Or even fellow Christians who have trouble with their temper;
We must bear critical remarks from those who should know better.
When those at work berate me or make me the butt of jokes,
I must bear it patiently as part of Jesus' yoke.
I can't be too offended when I think, to my disgrace,
How often I've offended Him who hung there in my place.

The "U" is the **Unfairness** of life's inequities,
How some are rich while some are poor, with patches on their knees,
And others run and jump in health, while others must remain
In hospitals and clinics, suffering every day in pain.

Some folks frolic in the sun, and sail in weather fair,
While others wrestle years before they see an answered prayer.
But let's have no self-pity, if to snivel I'm inclined,
For it wasn't fair for Jesus to be murdered by mankind!

I am no victim, but a Prince, and God will see me through,
And I can take it, I will make it; Jesus, I O U!

Manna Rained Around

Marching on toward Canaan Land, the Hebrews famished sore;
They wished for meat between their teeth and grumbled more and more.
God made quail, some three feet deep, to fall into their town…
They gorged on greasy gristle… while manna rained around!

The Prodigal stands desultory watch among the swine;
He's wasted his inheritance on women, song and wine…
So now he picks his kernels from the mire upon the ground.
He fills his belly with the husks, while manna rains around!

On the hills of Galilee, the thousands came to hear
The gracious words of Jesus as God's Kingdom drew quite near.
He multiplied the bread and fish that his disciples found,
But he really hoped they'd truly see that manna rained around!

Now a new millenium breaks wide across our shores,
And the "marchers on to Zion" are increasing by the scores.
So let's not spoil our dinner with the fast foods that abound;
Let's eat our fill of heaven's fare while manna rains around!

One Prayer

From the bowels of Hell came a pitiful wail
Above the roar of the flame:
"Why didn't I trust Jesus Christ as my Savior?
Why didn't I call on His name?

"When I was told that He died for my sin,
Why didn't I gratefully bow?
I'd give all the money I made on Earth
For a chance to receive him now!

"ONE PRAYER would have kept me out of this place:
'Lord Jesus, have mercy on me!'
Now what in the world was so all-fired important
That kept me from making that plea?"

Speak to the Rock

"Kiss the Son, lest he be angry, and you be destroyed in your way, for his wrath can flare up in a moment. Blessed are all who take refuge in him. "—Psalm 2:12

Thirsty and dry in the Sinai desert, the Israelites grumbled and fussed.
"Where is this famous 'Promised Land,' Moses?' All we see is dust."
Moses fell on his face to pray
That God would tell him what to say,
And the answer came in a very strange way:
"Speak, speak to the rock!"

For they had been to this place before, the Rock of Meribah.
The first time, he was told to strike the Rock with his wooden rod.
Weary and doubtful, Moses obeyed,
Wondering if this would make the grade,
Moses turned and struck it, and.... Say!
Water came forth from the Rock!

They'd wandered around in circles awhile, and now were back where they started.
They were even more tired and thirsty now, and even more downhearted.
Moses prayed, "Give me grace, I plead,
These people are ready to stone me, indeed!
Are you able to supply our needs?"
"Speak, speak to the Rock!"

Well, the grousers groused, and the moaners moaned, till Moses blew his
stack.
He said "You rebels, must we bring you water from out of this rock?"
He dealt the rock an angry blow,
And water flowed, but God said "WHOA!
You didn't do as I told you, Moe!
'Speak, speak to the Rock!'"

The lesson showed the people how that Christ would be struck for our sin.
The Suffering Servant, Messiah, the Lamb, would be stricken by wicked
men.
But then he would rise, as the Scriptures say,
And ever after, since that day,
We get to God by just one way....
"Speak! Speak to the Rock!"

Expectations

I wake up every morning expecting to be had,
If I am, its normal, and if I'm not, I'm glad.
It matters not if prices rise or wicked people win,
For God will give us what we need, whatever case we're in.

I wake up every morning expecting to be robbed,
If no, I can be happy; but if yes, I'll pray to God.
For thieves and robbers have no friends, they're on their own indeed,
While God sticks to me closer than a brother when in need.

I wake up every morning expecting to be blamed.
For maybe I deserve it, and if I am defamed,
It is a grim reminder I've an evil heart within,
But God is faithful to forgive those who confess their sin.

I wake up every morning expecting to be killed;
If no, I serve another day; if yes, I will be thrilled!
For I've a home in Heaven which was purchased there for me,
Because of Him who shed his blood for sinners on the Tree.

I wake up every morning expecting to be Raptured,
And fly with all my brethren whom by God have been recaptured,
And sing the song of angels, while I learn the mystery
That lies beyond this mortal coil, adorned in victory!

The Baton Keeper

The churches ran a relay race to see which was the fastest;
Where runners would pass off batons, the fourth would be the lastest.
Everyone in town turned out to see the churches race…
First Grace was favored big to win, they had the quickest pace.

Pastor Yorick, in his youth, had won olympic trials.
They called him "Hell in Track Shoes," 'cause he ran a wicked mile!
Still quick of mind and fleet of foot, he now would run first lap,
To build up an enormous lead that no one else could cap.

First runners to the blocks! "Get set!" The starter's gun went *bang*!
Muscles churning, cinders flying, Yorick led the gang!
Nobody could catch him with his streak-of-lightning burn…
The crowd cheered the old champion as he rounded the last turn…

The younger racers crouched in lane, they knew their turns were coming…
But instead of passing the baton, Old Yorick kept on running!
"Sir, come on! You have to pass!" the younger men did plead.
"No! You're inexperienced, and you might blow the lead!"

"It's my turn now!" said Durfy Dooner. "Let me run awhile!"
"I don't want to!" Yorick said. "You're gonna cramp my style!"
"You've run your lap; now by goshdarnit, give me that baton!"
"Are you saying I'm too old? Now just you watch me, son!"

"Sir, you've gone three laps yourself, now stop!" said Elbey Schmert,
Grabbing for the race baton, and poised for his grand spurt.
"You are weakly," Yorick said, "And you can't take the blows!
"I've won more races, sonny boy, than you've hairs in your nose!"

The cheers faded to silence as the fractious runners passed;
The crowd just placed their hands across their mouths and stood aghast
As three young men tugged after Yorick, making jabs and lurches;
It wasn't long before First Grace was passed by other churches.

At length his teammates all gave up, and there Old Yorick sat,
Sweating, panting on the cinders, grinning like a cat.
He showed up all those younger men, and to the last, hung on!
The race was lost, but at all costs, he sure kept that baton!

To Lois

The Bible says "men love your wives" and didn't say "sometimes,"
Like only when she understands, or passion rises high,
Or when the dinner's ready, or the money's there to spend;
I am resolved to do it, not just every now and then.

So no more fifty-fifty, but a hundred now you'll get…
And I'll be there to love and care, though times be rougher yet.
I'm done with all self-pity, no more acting like a jerk…
I'm here to say I love you, and I'm going to make it work.

You are the lady of my house, the one who shares my life,
The mother of our children and a doggone pretty wife.
So keep these verses handy for whenever we're apart,
For you're the one who turned my head, and the one who won my heart!